Resilience Series
BUG BYTES

ISBN 978-1-4341-0528-8

This book is made available in electronic form by the CISA, the Cybersecurity and Infra-structure Security Agency, which is a standalone United States federal agency, an operational component under Department of Homeland Security oversight. Its activities are a continuation of the National Protection and Programs Directorate:

https://www.cisa.gov/

As a U.S. government publication, this book is in the public domain. This printed edition is published by Waking Lion Press, an imprint of the Editorium. Waking Lion Press is not endorsed by or affiliated in any way with the CISA or the U.S. Department of Homeland Security.

Waking Lion Press™ and Editorium™ are trademarks of:

The Editorium, LLC
West Jordan, UT 84081-6132
www.editorium.com

CAN'T BELIEVE YOU'RE ALREADY IN GRAD SCHOOL! FIRST GRADUATING CUM LAUDE IN CYBERSECURITY, AND THEN YOU GOT THAT FULL RIDE TO GRAD SCHOOL FOR JOURNALISM! AND YOU'RE A TEACHING ASSISTANT TOO! YOU MAKE ME SO PROUD, KID!

THANKS, DAD!

C'MON SWEETHEART, IS THAT ALL YOU GOT FOR YOUR OLD MAN?! YOU EARNED THIS! YOU'RE THE FIRST OF US TO GET TO COLLEGE, LET ALONE GRAD SCHOOL.

NOW STOP ALREADY! YOU KNOW WHAT MOM WOULD HAVE SAID.

AAAAND THIS IS ME... GOTTA GO, DAD!

...SPECIAL BULLETIN AS COVID-19 NUMBERS CONTINUE TO RISE ACROSS THE NATION.

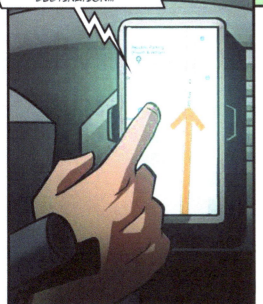

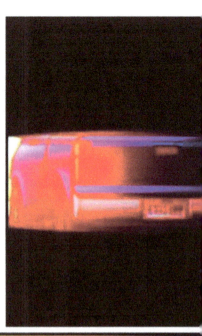

ALL CLEAR. WE HAD TO IMPROVISE A BIT. WE HAD SOME COMPANY. BUT HE WON'T BE ANY TROUBLE.

HEY, SWEETIE.

DAD? ARE YOU OK?

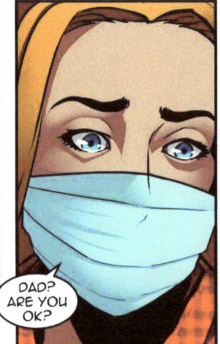

WHO COULD HAVE DONE THIS TO YOU?!

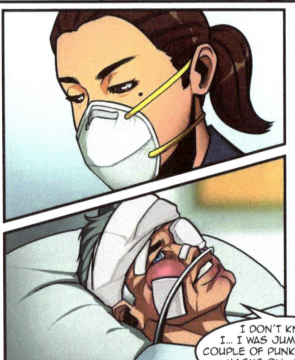

I DON'T KNOW... I... I WAS JUMPED BY A COUPLE OF PUNKS! THEY HAD MASKS ON...AND NOT THE GOOD KIND!

MA'AM, HE NEEDS TIME TO REST. PLEASE WAIT OUTSIDE.

SURE...

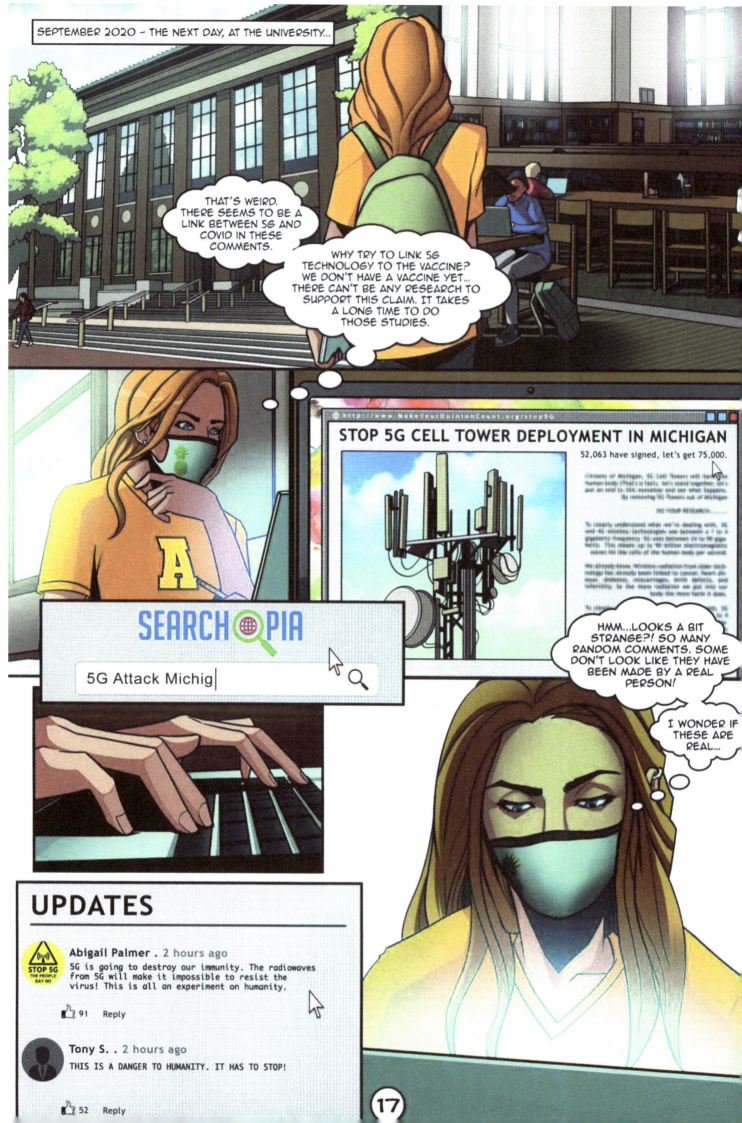

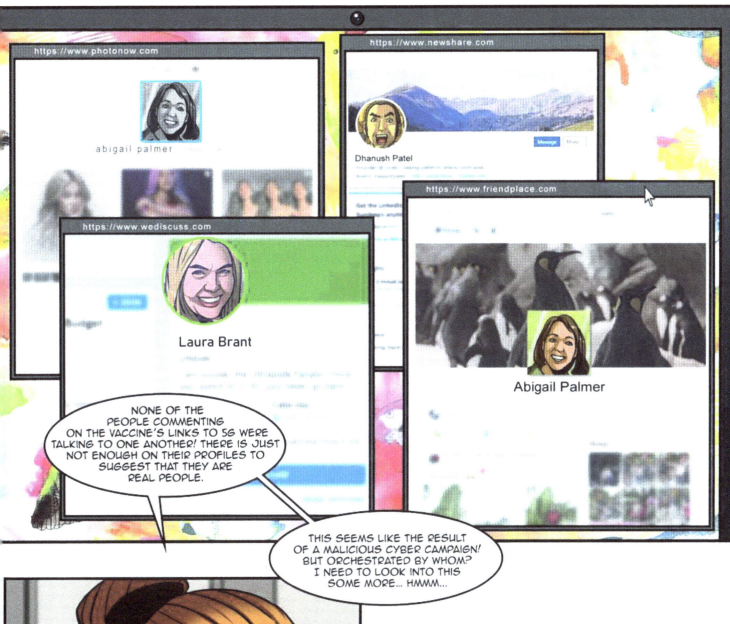

DAY TURNS INTO NIGHT.

SLEEP

SHUTDOWN

RESTART

LOG OFF

LAUNCH

THERE ARE SOME
TRACES ONLINE, BUT THEY NEVER TALK TO ONE
ANOTHER? THEY NEVER SEEM TO POST A
COMMENT AND HAVE A DISCUSSION WITH ONE
ANOTHER ON VERY OBVIOUSLY SHARED
IDEALS... SOMETHING FUNNY'S
GOING ON...

OFFICE

REMEMBERING COLLEEN, HER FRIEND FROM GRAD SCHOOL, AVA CALLS HER FOR THE CONTACT DETAILS OF A LAWYER THEY HAD PREVIOUSLY MET, WHO MAY BE ABLE TO HELP.

COLLEEN, CAN YOU PING ME THE NAME OF THAT LAWYER LADY WE MET FROM DC? THE ONE WHO KNOWS A LOT ABOUT CYBER LAWS AND DISINFORMATION. THANKS!

Sondra Jefferies

WOW, SHE SEEMS LIKE THE RIGHT PERSON. SHE PRACTICES CYBER LAW.

AND... HERE'S HER NUMBER... MAYBE SHE CAN HELP!

SONDRA HERE...

HI. THIS IS AVA WILLIAMS FROM THE UNIVERSITY OF ANN ARBOR'S JOURNALISM DEPARTMENT. WE PREVIOUSLY MET...

NOT INTERESTED!

NO! WAIT--

26

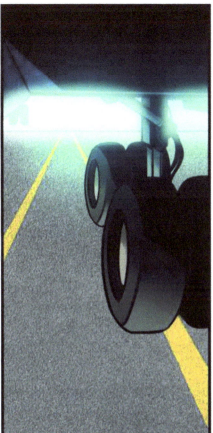

SCREEECH!

LADIES AND GENTLEMEN, WELCOME TO WASHINGTON DULLES INTERNATIONAL AIRPORT. THE LOCAL TIME IS 6:55 P.M.

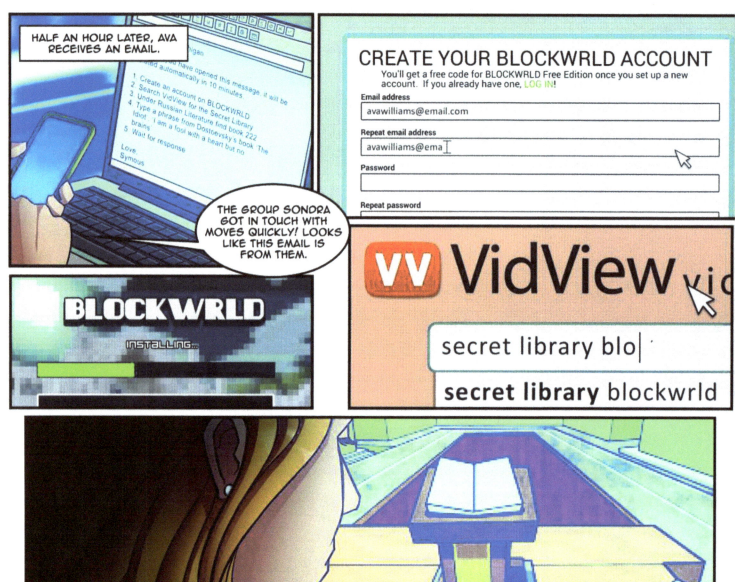

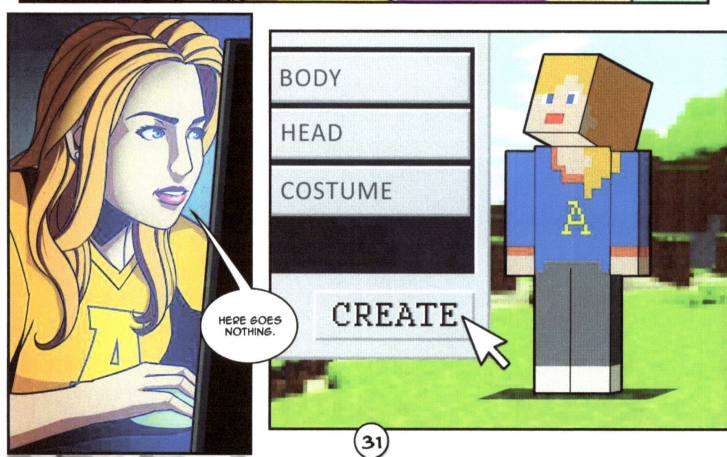

JAlanche ♥ ♥ ♥

AVA'S 3D AVATAR CLIMBS THE STAIRS OF THE SECRET LIBRARY.

AVAlanche ♥ ♥ ♥

RUSSIAN LITERATURE

SHE TOURS AROUND THIS VAST FACILITY, LOOKING AT OTHER 3D COUNTERPARTS AS WELL.

TAP!

ENTER

TAP! TAP! TAP!

CHAT BOX

I am a fool with a heart but no brains ▮

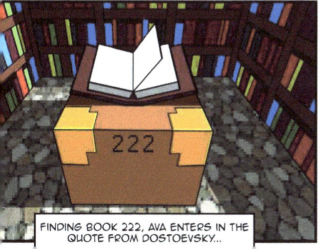

222

FINDING BOOK 222, AVA ENTERS IN THE QUOTE FROM DOSTOEVSKY...

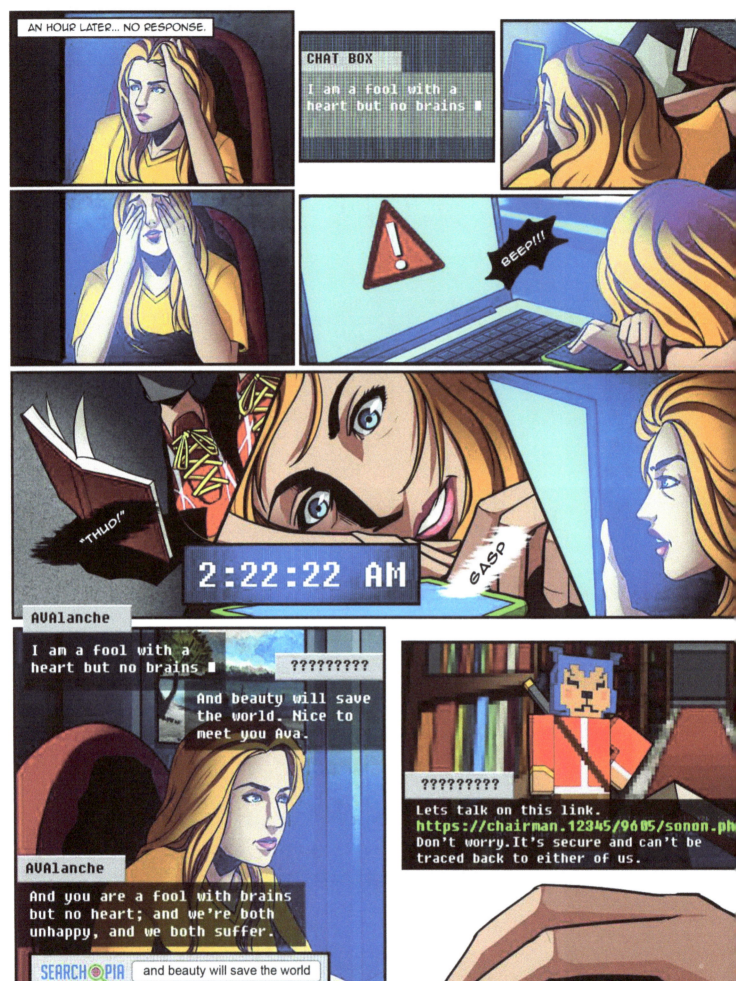

AN INTERNET PROTOCOL ADDRESS (IP ADDRESS) IS A NUMERICAL LABEL ASSIGNED TO EACH DEVICE CONNECTED TO A COMPUTER NETWORK THAT USES THE INTERNET PROTOCOL FOR COMMUNICATION. AN IP ADDRESS SERVES TWO MAIN FUNCTIONS: HOST OR NETWORK INTERFACE IDENTIFICATION AND LOCATION ADDRESSING.

From IP	To IP	OWNER
		"AX UKRAINE"
		"DIR RUSSIA"

WE HAVE THE VERY BEST WORKING WITH THE U.S. I'M QUITE CERTAIN THAT THE RUSSIANS HAVE BEEN TRYING TO DERAIL US FROM THE INSIDE OUT.

AND THEY DON'T NEED GUNS OR WEAPONS OF MASS DESTRUCTION TO PUT US ON THE PATH OF CHAOS. THEY JUST NEED YOUR SOCIAL MEDIA DATA.

MOSCOW IS SUPPLYING A LOAD OF NONSENSE TO A MULTITUDE OF ANTI-VACCINATION PETITIONS AND GROUPS. IT IS A TICKING TIME BOMB WHICH IS GOING TO BLOW UP IN OUR FACES UNLESS WE DO SOMETHING ABOUT IT!

A MAJOR CHALLENGE FACING US ALL TODAY IS THE INTEGRITY OF THE DATA WE ARE DROWNING IN. WHO IS BEHIND THE POST? IS THE SOCIAL MEDIA POST REAL? THIS IS THE DISINFORMATION PANDEMIC, AVA.

I HEAR YOU. I JUST DON'T KNOW WHAT I CAN DO TO HELP.

WHAT SOCIAL NETWORK EVEN HAS TIME FOR EXTENSIVE FACT CHECKING THESE DAYS? THE VELOCITY OF NEWS OUTSTRIPS HUMAN INTERVENTION AND THE AI WE HAVE CAN BE TRAINED, BUT IS NOT QUITE THERE YET.

HAS THERE BEEN ANY RESEARCH OR DATA THAT MAY HELP US DIFFERENTIATE BETWEEN THE ALGORITHMIC RESPONSES VERSUS THOSE BY THE TROLLS?

YOU NOTICED A PRETTY SIMPLE TIME TREND ON THAT PETITION. IT'S OFTEN WAY MORE COMPLEX. IT'S A PATTERN THE HUMAN EYE OFTEN MISSES AND SOMETIMES REQUIRES, SHALL WE SAY, "GOING THE EXTRA MILE."

ALSO, ONE OF OUR GUYS AT NICT PROVED THAT A BOT NEVER REPLIES TO ANOTHER BOT'S COMMENT.

IT'S TAKEN US YEARS TO DEVELOP THE RESOURCES AND CAPABILITY WE HAVE TODAY. THERE ARE MANY OF US LOOKING TO PROTECT WHAT WE LOVE. I WANT YOU TO JOIN THE FAMILY, AVA! WE ALL WANT THE SAME THING.

TOGETHER, WE CAN BUILD OUR GROUP OF DIGITAL PATRIOTS TO FACE THESE BAD ACTORS. AND MORE PEOPLE LIKE YOUR DAD CAN BE PROTECTED FROM THE FALLOUT OF WHAT IS LARGELY GOING UNNOTICED BY THE COUNTRY.

THIS IS BIGGER THAN ANYTHING I COULD HAVE ANTICIPATED. BUT, FORGIVE ME, ALL OF THIS FEELS LIKE A BAD DREAM! I DON'T EVEN KNOW WHO YOU ARE!

CHAIRMAN: Our secrecy is part of what keeps us all safe.

CHAIRMAN: We 'exist' in cyberspace. But should you choose to be our voice to the outside world, we can provide you with unparallelled resources to conduct your investigation. I'll leave you to it. You know what to do.

36

AVA BEGINS THE LONG JOURNEY FROM ANN ARBOR TO PARK COLLEGE UNIVERSITY.

AVA SPOTS A GAS STATION, SOMEWHERE CLOSE TO PITTSBURGH, ON HER GPS.

SHE STOPS TO TAKE A BREAK AND TO BUY SOME REFRESHMENTS.

AVA SPOTS THE SAME CAR SHE SAW EARLIER, PULL UP NEXT TO HER AT THE GAS STATION.

THAT'LL BE $7.50.

PING

THANKS.

AVA SPOTS TWO FIGURES ENTERING THE SHOP AND A WORRIED EXPRESSION APPEARS ACROSS HER FACE.

EXIT

WE LOST
HER!

SCREEEECH!

41

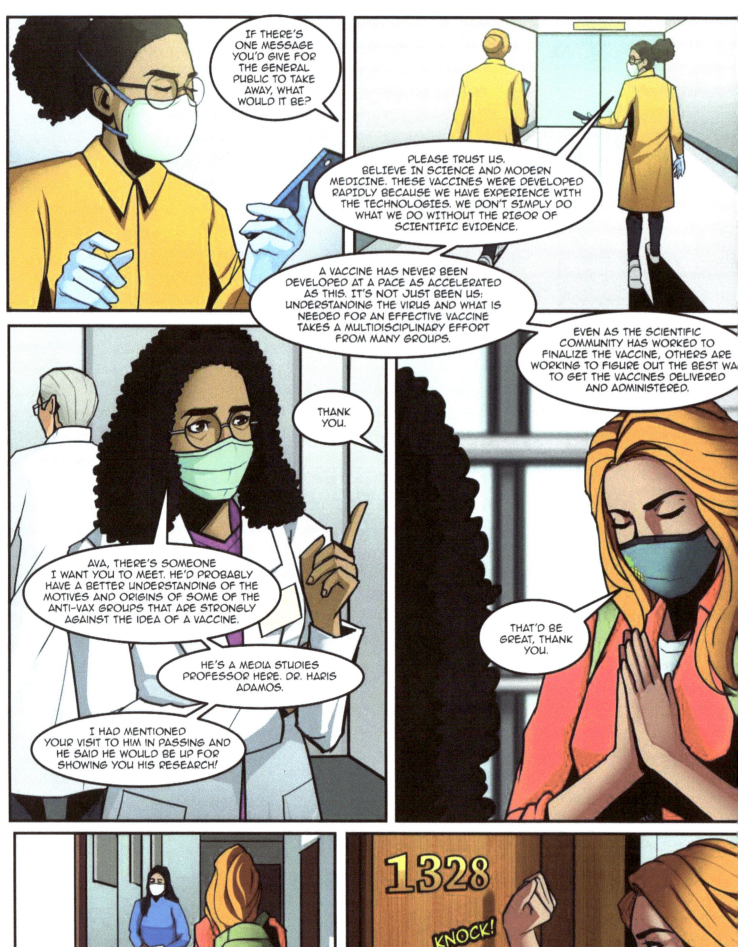

IF THERE'S ONE MESSAGE YOU'D GIVE FOR THE GENERAL PUBLIC TO TAKE AWAY, WHAT WOULD IT BE?

PLEASE TRUST US. BELIEVE IN SCIENCE AND MODERN MEDICINE. THESE VACCINES WERE DEVELOPED RAPIDLY BECAUSE WE HAVE EXPERIENCE WITH THE TECHNOLOGIES. WE DON'T SIMPLY DO WHAT WE DO WITHOUT THE RIGOR OF SCIENTIFIC EVIDENCE.

A VACCINE HAS NEVER BEEN DEVELOPED AT A PACE AS ACCELERATED AS THIS. IT'S NOT JUST BEEN US: UNDERSTANDING THE VIRUS AND WHAT IS NEEDED FOR AN EFFECTIVE VACCINE TAKES A MULTIDISCIPLINARY EFFORT FROM MANY GROUPS.

EVEN AS THE SCIENTIFIC COMMUNITY HAS WORKED TO FINALIZE THE VACCINE, OTHERS ARE WORKING TO FIGURE OUT THE BEST WA TO GET THE VACCINES DELIVERED AND ADMINISTERED.

THANK YOU.

AVA, THERE'S SOMEONE I WANT YOU TO MEET. HE'D PROBABLY HAVE A BETTER UNDERSTANDING OF THE MOTIVES AND ORIGINS OF SOME OF THE ANTI-VAX GROUPS THAT ARE STRONGLY AGAINST THE IDEA OF A VACCINE.

HE'S A MEDIA STUDIES PROFESSOR HERE. DR. HARIS ADAMOS.

I HAD MENTIONED YOUR VISIT TO HIM IN PASSING AND HE SAID HE WOULD BE UP FOR SHOWING YOU HIS RESEARCH!

THAT'D BE GREAT, THANK YOU.

1328

KNOCK!

KNOCK!

47

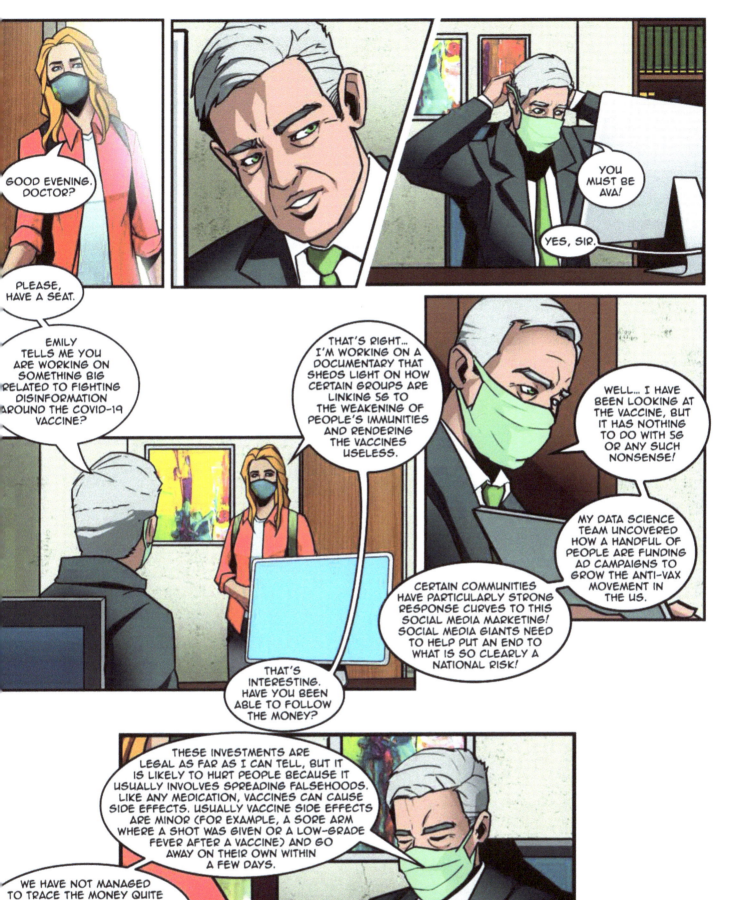

GOOD EVENING. DOCTOR?

YOU MUST BE AVA!

YES, SIR.

PLEASE, HAVE A SEAT.

EMILY TELLS ME YOU ARE WORKING ON SOMETHING BIG RELATED TO FIGHTING DISINFORMATION AROUND THE COVID-19 VACCINE?

THAT'S RIGHT... I'M WORKING ON A DOCUMENTARY THAT SHEDS LIGHT ON HOW CERTAIN GROUPS ARE LINKING 5G TO THE WEAKENING OF PEOPLE'S IMMUNITIES AND RENDERING THE VACCINES USELESS.

WELL... I HAVE BEEN LOOKING AT THE VACCINE, BUT IT HAS NOTHING TO DO WITH 5G OR ANY SUCH NONSENSE!

MY DATA SCIENCE TEAM UNCOVERED HOW A HANDFUL OF PEOPLE ARE FUNDING AD CAMPAIGNS TO GROW THE ANTI-VAX MOVEMENT IN THE US.

CERTAIN COMMUNITIES HAVE PARTICULARLY STRONG RESPONSE CURVES TO THIS SOCIAL MEDIA MARKETING! SOCIAL MEDIA GIANTS NEED TO HELP PUT AN END TO WHAT IS SO CLEARLY A NATIONAL RISK!

THAT'S INTERESTING. HAVE YOU BEEN ABLE TO FOLLOW THE MONEY?

THESE INVESTMENTS ARE LEGAL AS FAR AS I CAN TELL, BUT IT IS LIKELY TO HURT PEOPLE BECAUSE IT USUALLY INVOLVES SPREADING FALSEHOODS. LIKE ANY MEDICATION, VACCINES CAN CAUSE SIDE EFFECTS. USUALLY VACCINE SIDE EFFECTS ARE MINOR (FOR EXAMPLE, A SORE ARM WHERE A SHOT WAS GIVEN OR A LOW-GRADE FEVER AFTER A VACCINE) AND GO AWAY ON THEIR OWN WITHIN A FEW DAYS.

WE HAVE NOT MANAGED TO TRACE THE MONEY QUITE AS FAR AS I WOULD HAVE LIKED TO. SOME IS COMING FROM THE PRIVATE INVESTORS, BUT OTHERS, I AM NOT TOO SURE AT PRESENT.

IT'S A LABYRINTHINE NETWORK OF COMPANIES WHICH, IF I AM HONEST, IS NOT WHAT WE ARE SET UP TO LOOK AT... BUT IF YOU KNOW ANY FINANCIAL CRIME EXPERTS WHO HAVE MORE EXPERIENCE TRACKING THE FLOW OF MONEY, WHAT WE HAVE HERE MAY BE RIGHT UP THEIR ALLEY.

48

WHAT YOU ARE DOING... IT'S COMMENDABLE! I DO SEE THE NEED TO FIGHT AGAINST DISINFORMATION THAT COULD LEAD TO LOWER TAKE UP OF ANY VACCINE! I AM PARTICULARLY WORRIED ABOUT THE ANTI-VAX MOVEMENT.

YOU CANNOT USE SCIENTIFIC RATIONALITY AND NUMBERS TO WIN THIS WAR, AVA. YOU NEED TO WIN THEIR HEARTS AND MINDS FIRST AND THEN SHOW THEM THE TRUTH!... YOU DO HAVE CONCRETE PROOF, RIGHT? THAT THERE ARE GROUPS DELIBERATELY SETTING OUT TO INFLUENCE THEM?

I HAVE THE PROOF, DOCTOR! AND, TOGETHER WITH YOUR DATA, I THINK WE COULD MAKE SENSE OF IT ALL FOR THEM... I JUST NEED TO GET IN FRONT OF THEM.

THE OTHER CHALLENGE IS THAT YOU HAVE TO PERSUADE THEM THROUGH THEIR OWN MEDIA. THEY DON'T TRUST MAINSTREAM NEWS, AS I AM SURE YOU WELL UNDERSTAND. YOU WILL NEED TO MEET WITH DARREN LANCASTER, WHO LEADS TRUSTINNATURE, THE MOST POPULAR ANTI-VAX SITE, AND BE "INVITED" TO SHARE A STORY... AND THE IRREFUTABLE PROOF.

MY RESEARCH IS ALL OUT THERE ALREADY, BUT I AM SEEN AS TOO PRO-VAX TO HAVE A VOICE THERE!

OK, LET ME GET THAT FROM YOU!

WELL, I DID HAVE THIS INCREDIBLY... SHALL WE SAY "ANIMATED" DEBATE WITH DARREN OVER A TEXT WAR. LET ME SEE IF I CAN FIND HIS NUMBER... COULD GIVE YOU HIS -- AH! THERE IT IS... DARREN'S NUMBER...

I WILL SEND OVER THE DATA I HAVE TOO, SO THAT YOU CAN SHARE IT WITH DARREN. SHOW HIM THAT NONE OF THIS IS DOCTORED. THE ONLY THINGS MADE UP HERE ARE THOSE ADS!

THANK YOU DOCTOR. I REALLY APPRECIATE THIS!

CALL ME HARIS!

TAKE CARE AVA, AND GOOD LUCK.

I'LL DO MY BEST. SUCH A PLEASURE, HARIS.

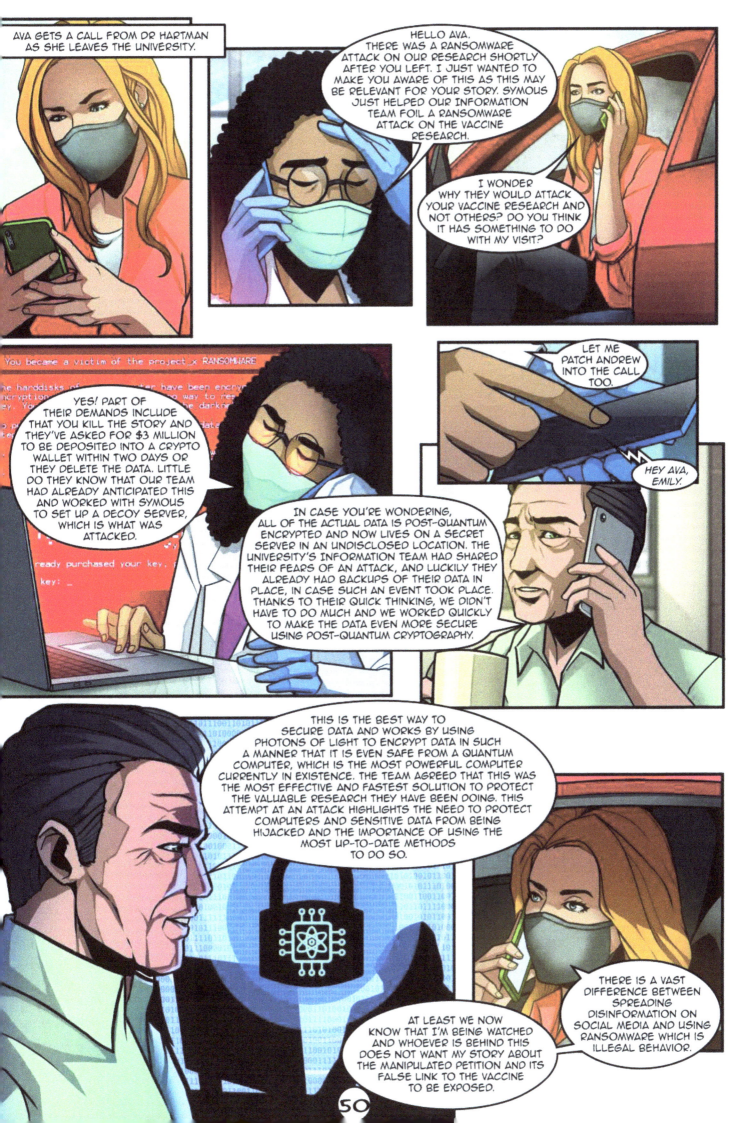

AVA GETS A CALL FROM DR HARTMAN AS SHE LEAVES THE UNIVERSITY.

HELLO AVA. THERE WAS A RANSOMWARE ATTACK ON OUR RESEARCH SHORTLY AFTER YOU LEFT. I JUST WANTED TO MAKE YOU AWARE OF THIS AS THIS MAY BE RELEVANT FOR YOUR STORY. SYMOUS JUST HELPED OUR INFORMATION TEAM FOIL A RANSOMWARE ATTACK ON THE VACCINE RESEARCH.

I WONDER WHY THEY WOULD ATTACK YOUR VACCINE RESEARCH AND NOT OTHERS? DO YOU THINK IT HAS SOMETHING TO DO WITH MY VISIT?

YES! PART OF THEIR DEMANDS INCLUDE THAT YOU KILL THE STORY AND THEY'VE ASKED FOR $3 MILLION TO BE DEPOSITED INTO A CRYPTO WALLET WITHIN TWO DAYS OR THEY DELETE THE DATA. LITTLE DO THEY KNOW THAT OUR TEAM HAD ALREADY ANTICIPATED THIS AND WORKED WITH SYMOUS TO SET UP A DECOY SERVER, WHICH IS WHAT WAS ATTACKED.

IN CASE YOU'RE WONDERING, ALL OF THE ACTUAL DATA IS POST-QUANTUM ENCRYPTED AND NOW LIVES ON A SECRET SERVER IN AN UNDISCLOSED LOCATION. THE UNIVERSITY'S INFORMATION TEAM HAD SHARED THEIR FEARS OF AN ATTACK, AND LUCKILY THEY ALREADY HAD BACKUPS OF THEIR DATA IN PLACE, IN CASE SUCH AN EVENT TOOK PLACE. THANKS TO THEIR QUICK THINKING, WE DIDN'T HAVE TO DO MUCH AND WE WORKED QUICKLY TO MAKE THE DATA EVEN MORE SECURE USING POST-QUANTUM CRYPTOGRAPHY.

LET ME PATCH ANDREW INTO THE CALL TOO.

HEY AVA, EMILY.

THIS IS THE BEST WAY TO SECURE DATA AND WORKS BY USING PHOTONS OF LIGHT TO ENCRYPT DATA IN SUCH A MANNER THAT IT IS EVEN SAFE FROM A QUANTUM COMPUTER, WHICH IS THE MOST POWERFUL COMPUTER CURRENTLY IN EXISTENCE. THE TEAM AGREED THAT THIS WAS THE MOST EFFECTIVE AND FASTEST SOLUTION TO PROTECT THE VALUABLE RESEARCH THEY HAVE BEEN DOING. THIS ATTEMPT AT AN ATTACK HIGHLIGHTS THE NEED TO PROTECT COMPUTERS AND SENSITIVE DATA FROM BEING HIJACKED AND THE IMPORTANCE OF USING THE MOST UP-TO-DATE METHODS TO DO SO.

AT LEAST WE NOW KNOW THAT I'M BEING WATCHED AND WHOEVER IS BEHIND THIS DOES NOT WANT MY STORY ABOUT THE MANIPULATED PETITION AND ITS FALSE LINK TO THE VACCINE TO BE EXPOSED.

THERE IS A VAST DIFFERENCE BETWEEN SPREADING DISINFORMATION ON SOCIAL MEDIA AND USING RANSOMWARE WHICH IS ILLEGAL BEHAVIOR.

50

ONE WEEK LATER, IN THE MEDIA RECORDING LAB IN THE UNIVERSITY.

PLEASURE TO HAVE YOU WITH US, DARREN. LET'S DIVE RIGHT IN... CAN YOU TELL ME A LITTLE MORE ABOUT YOUR ROLE AT TRUSTINNATURE?

SURE. I HEAD UP THE NATION'S LARGEST DIGITAL ANTI-VAX COMMUNITY. WE HAV OVER 15 MILLION MEMBERS AROUND THE NATION!

THAT'S QUITE A FOOTPRINT. WHAT IS THE CORE REASON YOU'RE AGAINST VACCINATION?

PERSONALLY, DO YOU THINK THE VERY IDEA OF GOVERNMENT ORGANIZATIONS IN THE HEALTH SECTOR PROMOTING VACCINES IS WRONG?

YES, I DO THINK IT'S WRONG. THE INFLUENZA VACCINE HAS NOT QUITE WORKED.

MUCH OF WHAT WE SEE BEING PEDDLED BY THE GOVERNMENT IS PSEUDOSCIENCE WITH INCONCLUSIVE DATA SUPPORTING THEIR HYPOTHESIS. WE HAVE OUR OWN SCIENCE TEAMS THAT HAVE SHOWN THAT THE DATA ITSELF IS QUESTIONABLE AROUND HOW WELL THESE NEW VACCINES WORK! OUR BACKERS BELIEVE IN OUR MISSION TOO. WE ARE HERE TO PROTECT AMERICA.

LIKE I SAID EARLIER AND AS WE CAN NOW SEE, VACCINES AREN'T PERFECT. THEY'RE NOT EVEN FREE!

DO YOU EVER THINK WHATEVER YOU BELIEVE COULD AT LEAST BE REMOTELY CONNECTED TO DISINFORMATION OR SOME SOCIAL MEDIA WILDFIRE?

LIVE

Ava Williams

2003

EVEN IF IT IS TRUE, I STILL BELIEVE IT'S THE SELFISHNESS OF THE SYSTEM. AND FOR WHAT? THE NEWS AND EVIDENCE IS THERE.

WHAT IF IT'S NOT GENUINE?

MANY DISEASES HAVE BEEN ELIMINATED FROM THIS COUNTRY, SO WHY PERPETUATE THE VICIOUS CYCLE? FLU SHOTS HAVE EVEN BEEN CORRELATED TO INFLUENZA IN THE PAST.

SO ARE WE GOING TO KEEP GIVING MAINSTREAM MEDIA TOTAL POWER?

THERE ARE MANY INTERVENTIONS THAT DON'T INVOLVE A VACCINE... HERD IMMUNITY IS A THING, RIGHT?

BUT WHAT ABOUT COVID-19? IT'S A DISEASE NO ONE HAS REALLY HEARD OF TILL NOW.

DON'T PEOPLE DIE EVERY DAY? NO ONE BATS AN EY WAR, POVERTY, CORRUP' WE HAVEN'T EVEN BEEN TO ERADICATE INFLUE' FOR CRYING OUT LOUD.

DON'T YOU THINK THERE'LL BE TOO MANY DEATHS BEFORE WE REACH THAT?

WE HAVE SOME HARD SACRIFICES TO MAKE. ALL THE VACCINES AMERICAN KIDS HAVE BEEN HIT WITH, DON'T YOU BELIEVE WE'VE BEEN CLOGGING UP THEIR IMMUNE SYSTEMS?

WHAT ABOUT THE FACTS AND STATISTICS ORGANIZATIONS LIKE THE UNITED NATIONS PUBLISH?

JUST BECAUSE IT'S A NUMBER DOESN'T MEAN IT'S TRUE. DON'T YOU THINK METRICS ARE USED TO PUSH AN AGENDA, UNDER A COVER OF BEING OBJECTIVE? WE NEED TO LISTEN TO THE PUBLIC, AND WITH SEVERAL MILLION VOTERS AS MEMBERS, WE THINK THAT TRUSTINNATURE HAS THE POTENTIAL TO BE AN IMPORTANT VOICE IN THE SPACE. WHY NOT THE SAME HERE? PARENTS HAVE TO BE ABLE TO DECIDE FOR THEIR CHILDREN, NOT THE GOVERNMENT. WHAT PARENT WOULD WANT THEIR KIDS TO BE PLAGUED BY AUTISM OR ARTHRITIS? APPARENTLY, IT SEEMS THAT WAY, GIVEN THE BILLION DOLLARS' WORTH OF MARKETING THESE MEDICAL COMPANIES INVEST IN.

SPEAKING OF MARKETING DOLLARS, IT APPEARS AS IF YOUR GROUP IS ONE OF THE TWO SPENDING TENS OF MILLIONS ON DIGITAL ADVERTISING ON FRIENDPLACE AND OTHER PLATFORMS? CAN YOU ELABORATE ON YOUR DONOR BASE?

NO COMMENT ON OUR DONORS. SOME ARE PUBLIC AND OTHERS PREFER TO BE KEPT OUT OF THE SPOTLIGHT. SO, IN DEFERENCE TO THEIR PRIVACY, LET'S PLEASE MOVE TO THE NEXT QUESTION. BUT "YES," TO ANSWER YOUR QUESTION, WE ARE SPENDING ON DIGITAL ADVERTISING AS IT SEEMS TO BE THE BEST WAY TO GROW OUR BASE.

55

SANCHEZ FAMILY, WE ARE READY FOR YOU!

PREPARATIONS FOR THE NEXT SEGMENT BEGIN.

AVA HAS REMOVED HER MASK, AS SHE EXITS THE BUILDING.

Hey Ava, this is the chairman. That went about as well as could be expected :) Message me here when you are done. I have some news for you!

Feels creepy that you are always watching.

Just remember... we are not the only ones watching.

HELLO, CHAIRMAN.

LOOKS LIKE WE ARE MAKING SOME HEADWAY.

YES. I THINK IT'S GOING WELL. WE NEED TO SEED THAT INTERVIEW AS WIDELY ACROSS THE INTERNET AS POSSIBLE. AND I KNOW THAT TRUSTINNATURE WILL COVER IT AS LANCASTER IS ON IT. I MADE SOME TIME TO SPEAK TO THE CHIEF AT MARYLAND.

WE HAVE DONE WHAT WE NEEDED TO DO AND OUR INFLUENCERS HAVE BEEN PAID TO SEED YOUR SEGMENT ACROSS EVERY MAJOR SOCIAL MEDIA CHANNEL. YOUR INTERVIEW IS ALREADY BLOWING UP ALL OVER THE WEB. AND THE PETITION IS GETTING HEAT!

NO WONDER MY PHONE IS PINGING LIKE CRAZY. I HAD TO TURN OFF NOTIFICATIONS!!

THAT IS THE POWER OF THE NEW NORMAL WHEN IT COMES TO NEWS. IT CUTS BOTH WAYS. THE TROLLS HAVE ALSO STARTED TO FIGHT BACK. BUT TOO MANY INDEPENDENT GROUPS ARE RUNNING THE DATA. YOUR CONCLUSIONS HAVE ALREADY BEEN CONFIRMED BY MEDIA, INDEPENDENT BLOGGERS AND FOREIGN CORRESPONDENTS. NOW WE WAIT AND SEE WHAT HAPPENS. I EXPECT SOME PUSHBACK!

SHOULD I BE WORRIED?

DON'T WORRY, YOU WILL HAVE SUPPORT AND A PRIVATE DETAIL.

THANKS, AND WILL DO. I DON'T KNOW HOW TO THANK YOU!

I THINK SOMEONE IS WAITING FOR YOU AT HOME. WHY DON'T WE TOUCH BASE AFTER? AND DON'T WORRY, HE IS IN VERY GOOD HANDS!

56

EW MONTHS LATER —AVA ARRIVES AT THE NATIONAL JOURNALISM AWARD CEREMONY.

NATIONAL JOURNALISM AWARDS

THE PAPARAZZI IS PRESENT AND AVA SEES SOME FAMILIAR FACES.

OUR FINAL AWARD FOR "BEST NEWCOMER AND USE OF DIGITAL MEDIA" GOES TO SOMEONE WHOSE WORK HAS BEEN INSTRUMENTAL IN EDUCATING PEOPLE DURING A TIME WHERE DISINFORMATION IS RAMPANT AND PEOPLE ARE QUICK TO BELIEVE NEWS WITHOUT VERIFYING ITS ACCURACY.

THE CEREMONY IS THIS WAY, MISS WILLIAMS.

THE AWARD GOES TO MISS AVA WILLIAMS!

AVA GOES ON STAGE TO COLLECT HER AWARD.

NATIONAL JOURNALISM AWARDS

BEST NEWCOMER and USE OF DIGITAL MEDIA

SHE HAS DONE GREAT WORK AROUND HIGHLIGHTING THE BENEFITS OF A VACCINE WHICH WILL COUNTER THE VIRUS AND ENCOURAGING PEOPLE TO EXPLORE DIFFERING VIEWPOINTS. MOST NOTABLY, HER WORK RESULTED IN A TIP-OFF THAT THWARTED AN ATTACK ON AN IMPORTANT VACCINE STOCKPILE.

WE OWE MISS WILLIAMS A LOT OF GRATITU FOR HER EFFORTS AND SH IS A VERY WORTHY RECIPIEN OF THIS AWARD.

THANK YOU. IT'S A GREAT HONOR TO RECEIVE THIS AWARD.

THE INTERNET SEES A HUGE VOLUME AND VARIETY OF INFORMATION PASS THROUGH IT EVERY DAY. POLITICALLY, SOCIALLY OR ECONOMICALLY WE WILL PROBABLY DISAGREE ON A LOT OF THINGS. BUT THERE IS NO PLACE FOR DISINFORMATION IN OUR LIVES.

AS SOMEONE WHO IS JUST STARTING MY CAREER AS A JOURNALIST, I AM HONORED AND EXCITED TO BE A PART OF A FIELD DEDICATED TO HOLDING OURSELVES AND OUR INSTITUTIONS ACCOUNTABLE. PEOPLE CAN GET INFORMATION FROM MANY PLACES THESE DAYS, MAKING OUR ABILITY TO EDUCATE THE PUBLIC THROUGH ACCURATE, FAIR, AND FACTUAL REPORTING EVEN MORE IMPORTANT.

MANY OF US ARE WORKING TO FIGHT DISINFORMATION. I THANK YOU FOR RECOGNIZING MY EFFORTS AND AM GRATEFUL TO HAVE HAD THE OPPORTUNITY TO HAVE PLAYED A SMALL PART IN A MUCH BIGGER STORY.

THANK YOU!

CISA ENCOURAGES EVERYONE TO CONSUME
INFORMATION WITH CARE. PRACTICING MEDIA
LITERACY INCLUDING VERIFYING SOURCES, SEEKING
ALTERNATIVE VIEWPOINTS, AND FINDING TRUSTED
SOURCES OF INFORMATION IS THE MOST EFFECTIVE
STRATEGY IN LIMITING THE EFFECT OF
DISINFORMATION. FOR MORE INFORMATION AND
FURTHER READING ABOUT DISINFORMATION, PLEASE
VISIT THE CYBERSECURITY & INFRASTRUCTURE
SECURITY AGENCY WEBSITE, WWW.CISA.GOV.

NOTES FROM CISA

DISINFORMATION IS AN EXISTENTIAL THREAT TO THE UNITED STATES, OUR DEMOCRATIC WAY OF LIFE, AND THE INFRASTRUCTURE ON WHICH IT RELIES. THE RESILIENCE SERIES (OF WHICH THIS IS THE SECOND TITLE) USES THE GRAPHIC NOVEL FORMAT TO COMMUNICATE THE DANGERS AND RISKS ASSOCIATED WITH DIS- AND MISINFORMATION THROUGH FICTIONAL STORIES THAT ARE INSPIRED BY REAL-WORLD EVENTS.

THE RESILIENCE SERIES GRAPHIC NOVELS WERE COMMISSIONED BY THE CYBERSECURITY AND INFRASTRUCTURE SECURITY AGENCY (CISA) TO SHARE INFORMATION TO ILLUSTRATE:

1) FOREIGN ACTORS ARE TRYING TO INFLUENCE U.S. SECURITY, ECONOMY, AND POLITICS THROUGH THE MALICIOUS USE OF ONLINE MEDIA TO CREATE AND AMPLIFY DISINFORMATION.

2) WHILE THE STRATEGY OF USING INACCURATE INFORMATION TO WEAKEN AND DIVIDE A SOCIETY IS NOT NEW, THE INTERNET AND SOCIAL MEDIA ALLOW DISINFORMATION TO SPREAD MORE QUICKLY THAN IT HAS IN THE PAST.

3) DEEPFAKES, BOTS, AND TROLL FARMS ARE JUST SOME OF THE EMERGING TECHNIQUES FOR CREATING AND SPREADING DISINFORMATION.

BIBLIOGRAPHY

PAGE 46:
J. WOLFE, "CORONAVIRUS BRIEFING: WHAT
HAPPENED TODAY," 2020
HTTPS://WWW.NYTIMES.COM/20
20/11/16/US/CORONAVIRUS-TODAY.HTML

PAGE 50:
S. GHOSE, "ARE YOU READY FOR THE QUANTUM
COMPUTING REVOLUTION?" 2020
HTTPS://HBR.ORG/2020/09/ARE-YOU-READY-FOR-T
HE-QUANTUM-COMPUTING-REVOLUTION

www.ingramcontent.com/pod-product-compliance
Lightning Source LLC
Chambersburg PA
CBHW040953050326
40689CB00028B/4986